THE MALLARMÉ POEMS

MATTHEW JARVIS

Cinnamon Press
:: small miracles from distinctive voices ::

Published by Cinnamon Press
Meirion House,
Glan yr afon,
Tanygrisiau
Blaenau Ffestiniog,
Gwynedd, LL41 3SU
www.cinnamonpress.com

British Library Cataloguing in Publication Data. A CIP record for this book can be obtained from the British Library.

Designed and typeset in Palatino by Cinnamon Press.

Cover design by Adam Craig. including masque image: ID 137691992 © Aleksei Iatsenko I Dreamstime.com

Cinnamon Press is represented in the UK by Inpress Ltd and in Wales by the Books Council of Wales.

Acknowledgements

'Speak Easy' has previously appeared in *Poetry Wales*.

'All Gone Swanless' was longlisted for the 2015 National Poetry Competition.

I am profoundly grateful to Gavin Goodwin, Jonathan Edwards, and Patrick McGuinness for encouragement and support.

Contents

For Kate, Dan, and Ethan

The Mallarmé Poems

Being Thirteen Free Improvisations on Lines from Mallarmé

1. Caxton! my Caxton!

'et j'ai lu tous les livres' (and I have read all the books)—Mallarmé

Books? Oh, if you must. But so dusty, so
dry, the page already read, the ink itself
worn faint by my recurrent eyes. Those
spectacles of words all long since hollowed
out, reduced at every thought to one stale
note, the thinnest scratch, a croak.

You'd never catch me reading now,
treading the well-scuffed path at the
page's perpetual turn. Get that book
off my desk! Leave the polished wood pris-
tine, untroubled by your high-piled spines,
by sentences that mutter in their dark
like muted choirs in constant discontent.

No, I'm all done with books. I've had my
fill—though still a library's quiet is good
for sleep, for public warmth beyond the cold
that slips its blade beneath your coat. But
books themselves? They're nothing to me
now, just re-runs, returns, the already-been-
said. I'd rather drink, for sure, or lie in bed.

2. All Gone Swanless

'Quelconque une solitude / Sans le cigne ni le quai' (Some unremarkable solitude / without swan or pier)—Mallarmé

Without a swan, there's just one word: un-
done. The height of fun all lost, all joys fore-
gone. Less hiss, less flap, less jabbing beak—all
true. But that lost white and I'm entirely
bl... oh, nothing, nothing more will do. The water-
side now bleakly grey, and I, gone swanless,
cannot bear the bitter, raw, unfeathered day.

But maybe night, high gaudy plumed in coloured
lights, in slot-machines, in giddy sights of shoot-
'em-ups—perhaps the night will clean the slate
this day has smudged, and fill the swannish
void. At least, it should be tried. But lights are
out, the dark entirely deep. No penny-push, no
arcade cars. I weep. The very pier itself ex-
tinguished, raptured, or—to put it simply—gawn.

My peerless swan! This pierless night! And I—new born
to sadness, solitude, grief—see all my pleasures torn.

3. Shadowed

'je vais voir l'ombre que tu devins' (I'll see the shadow that you became)—
Mallarmé

What did you do? I saw you fully formed, your
footprint firmed the sand, your voice resound-
ing vibrant, clear, from rock to mirrored
rock. I swear: the many-browned twists of your
hair—all there; and then lost to sudden
air. What? Where? I have spun my sight about
and am sure I saw a flicker, far out—a hint perhaps
of how you smile. There was something in that dip
of wave, that twist and flow of tide, that widely salt
suggestion of how you sometimes call my name.

Your shadow slips to my elbow now. You're just
the same. It's been no sort of change—although, of
course, you slide unpaid into concerts and resorts, while
your blunt retorts are rather more *implied*. Snide? Oh,
still. And, well, it's an act of will to lose to you at
cards. But at night, with the duvet and the sheets—
your formless form, the echo of an arm: there's
never calm; no peace; and nothing's warm.

4. Dough

'Et surtout ne va pas, mon frère, acheter du pain.' (And above all, my brother, do not go to buy bread) — Mallarmé

I tell you: this is no time for bread. Just clear
your head of flour, of crafted loaves, the strict
perfection of crust, the high-heat sweetness
of ovened bliss. I know those eyes, far-focused,
dreaming yeast, the rhythmed muscle of dough-in-the-
fist. You are, my brother, aroma's highest priest.

But this is no time to be sweetly lost. You must break
your dream against profit, the ledger — realpolitik, not
your heart's great hope, your pearl of great price, your
treasure. Oh my brother! Do not buy bread. That trap,
that snare. And this is no time for hope, mon frère.

5. Solo

'Oui, c'est pour moi, pour moi, que je fleuris, déserte!' (Yes, it's for me, for me, that I flower in solitude)—Mallarmé

Yes, for myself. Thus shall I spurn the door, ig-
nore the drummed knock, the bell—that chim-
ing death-knell ringing chaos to my head. No,
give me instead the tight acre of my narrow
bed. And duvet-spun to warmth, let me remain un-
caught in that twinned mess of legs, of palming
hands, of sex, so I may sleep unchecked, lost deep
in deepest quiet, in this vast and single dark.

So you can take your charm, your talk, your reek
of company. I will not break. I will be solitary, em-
brace my cell. But you: you are crowds, the scent
of cities, the threat of conversation, of colleagues'
bantered wit thrown fast from the keyboard's edge.
Stand back. Rescind your claimed affection. For you
are duplication, and in such doubling, my negation.

6. Snakey Snakey

'J'occupe mon antique soin' (I work on my ancient plan) —Mallarmé

Long in the making. That dry desire corroding
the gut; the spit of hate in your stomach's pit; the
knife that sang through the pulsing throat. So easy
have I bloomed despair, caught your kindnesses
at the root, by the hair; twisted hard until you
turned, found anger, moaned at what you'd lost,
what you'd become…but planned, nonetheless,
her hard landing, his sharp death, the killer word
delivered soft and laughing. Oh I have snaked

years since Eden, and vast my tracts of garden now.
How I have appled you, shackled you sweet on my
flickered tongue. So hang your head. Know you've
been done. Strung up. Outwitted at every turn. Just

burned. For I am always and ever—the venom you
never quite learned how to hide. Put escape from
your mind. I am here, hissing quiet, by your side.

7. In Memoriam: Human

'La pénultième est morte' (The penultimate is dead) —Mallarmé

And now there's only me. He lasted longer than
the rest, the rushing of his chest kept labouring
on as death herself pushed in and he thrashed
back each thickening breath. But in his evening,
rattling, he drifted off—my final company finally
done. So I'll go solitary on, I guess...well unless
his ghost comes taunting back, to spook me like
some hollow god playing Eden's voice to my Adam
in reverse. But would it be curse or blessing, that
spectral muttering tagged at my heels, chittering
by my ears, tracking my path through these numb
and shattered cities where we tumbled so fast to
our vanishing? Whatever: come haunt me; keep
talking. For already the words are diminishing: the
streets, the boutiques where we used to meet—
they are shedding their names, making blanks, dis-

engaging. But maybe that's my reason for remaining.
To lose our labels, re-shelve our words: to un-Adam
all the worlds we'd looped into language, that we'd
trapped in our chatter, made chattels. So no, muttering
ghost, don't bother: I'll just let it slide, glide off into
silence; I'll fade, turn skull, leave my mouth wide open—
a cave not for speaking but for soil, and the weather.

8. Howl

'Que de longues journées j'ai passées seul avec mon chat' (What long days I've spent alone with my cat)—Mallarmé

Well met, furball. Your call for mate or
fight has torn my sleep. So tell me, small
god, brief deity of fuzz and claw: what
service may I perform you, what chore, to
ease the toil of night-watch prowls, of your
mouse-kill working dim alleyways, of all that
prey played long and late bitten at the neck?

Purr-deep godling, here at least's my lap. So
nap your warmth. Source strength at this soft
altar for your fiercest tyrannies on rodent and on
bird, on insurgents both tabby and grey. Go
twitch-dream your mighty paw at those saps
of garden and of copse, no lapse from your
jaws, with all your furies of scratch and holler.

Old fleabag: you have stalked my days, to
whip me to your designations, to your ways,
to your feasts at kill and sleep. But would you
ditch me yet for sweeter cream, for more fresh
meat? I would be lost. Nonplussed. Altogether
glum. No: curl your tail upon my wrist. I will yet
serve your worship, as I've always done.

9. Clocked

'*Cette pendule de Saxe, qui retarde et sonne treize heures*' (*That Dresden clock, which runs slow and strikes thirteen*)—Mallarmé

So what's the actual point of you? Few
jobs, just tock and tick—and even that's
too much. Are you sick? Has your flock of
seconds run amok, escaped the shepherd's
crook of winder and of cogs? Milk was all I
wanted. But when it counted, when I trusted
your open face—I was late, disgraced, my
chase cut off, the shop locked up and dark.

And thirteen? Are you certain you're not
drunk—striking extras; making time of
bakers' dozens; preening all your great-
er minutes through the day's temporal

streets? But wait. I'll take that one more
hour on every twelve. Oh, at a shot. What's
not to like? Sneak in more sleep, more
chance for aimless drift, for thriftless spend,
for day's-end dreaming all my pointless
lusts and fancies of toyed-with dalliance,

romances. Though hold on. No. I can see
how it would really go: every second added
would gutter down to work, would shutter to a
reckoning with the dark. So keep your extra
hours. I'll stick to twenty-four. It's time, old clock,
to chuck you in a cupboard, lock the door.

10. Speak Easy

'lambeaux maudits d'une phrase absurde' (cursed shreds of an absurd phrase)—
Mallarmé

I didn't catch your drift. You spoke as someone
laughed and what you meant was lost, just
fragments of a speech left jagged on the air. So
now I'm cursing mirth, the giggle that strangled your
words. And yet—your face, expectant, urging my
reply... But how? There's only jangled sound; that
sentence come unstuck, unglued; conversation's
blown fuse. What can I do? Your words—they
flew diffused, in pieces, all their airs and graces
trampled, their presence abused, misdirected.

But who am I kidding? As if words ever did clear
bidding, budding rather into messages you never
thought or wrote, tumbling out of line, refusing to
beat time, holding you hostage or by the throat. So,
yes, you spoke. But even unimpeded your meaning
might have choked, chucked stones at sense, re-
fused to condense in the brain's deep ear. Oh, sure,
I'll try to hear: you speak again, I'll listen close. Chase
up suggestions, implications; parse every clause you
utter. Commit myself to all the flows, all the vagaries
of chatter. To all that clutter of the open mouth. But
don't hold out much hope. The words you say will
run, they'll play, they'll turn in their own way, threat-
en violence to each carefully crafted sentence. Oh
to hell with it. I give up. The only answer's silence.

11. The All-New Spiderman

'Ne songe pas aux toils d'araignées qui tremblent au haut des grandes croissées' (Don't dream about the spiderwebs which tremble at the top of the big casement windows) — Mallarmé

So now, scuttler, all dainty with your running: spun thick
that high ledge where you web your weaving, set ten-
sioned deaths for moth and fly, dance fine upon these fierce
wires of your home flung wide. Oh don't disappear, don't
hide in shy retreat. Yes, you carry a freight of shrieks, of
fear. But here? No. Be welcome. I'll give you warmth, con-
versation. And at my day's-end homing, in the closing
dark, I'll pat the cushion by my side, invite your attention,
proffer some devotion. So we will sit, convivial, batting talk
about. You'll fess up to the stress of spinning, to all that
work of flitting fast from prey so neatly trapped, from death
so tightly wrapped, to eggs resting quiet at a smudged
window's edge. And me? I'll weep my latest fudge, an-
other office bullet barely dodged; I'll shake my weak-
ling fist at advancement lost, at others rising fast while I,
tattered, end up scuppered, mentioned with a sneering in
despatches. Then we'll nod, consult our watches, concede
the danger of catches spilled, of chances killed by blunder.
And you'll settle for a moment on my shoulder, before
I slouch off to my half-earned slumber. So, please: don't

skulk around your dustball pelmet, arachnid, my room-
mate. Crawl down. Your webs are safe. I've banned the
hoover's reaching snout from the ceiling and its corners;
there'll be no more suction, fierce and searching, to fall
upon the quiet, hidden crawlers. From now on let us, mut-
ual, hold this place; and I will icon all your spin-thread grace.

17

12. Tea-Leaf

'un crime n'est pas bien difficile à faire' (committing a crime isn't difficult)—
Mallarmé

It's always so hard to resist: the hidden
gum held tight in the fist, the mag stuffed
fast under jumper or coat, pressed secret
and hard to the chest. Your trembling hand
on the filch, grabbing some fix of con-
traband. But no. That itch isn't worth the
scratch. Stay untouched, aloof: give the
cameras a face of innocence, truth. What's

the use of such small loot? I'd root every
time for a bigger gig: think heist at the
least. Outwitting vaults and computers,
both; staking out turf of bullion, gems, the
assets of banks too huge to end. Just re-
fuse to be sent down for less than ten
mill. Is that worth the buzz, the thrill? I
wonder. Let's dream you larger still. Think

grander. Plan vast. Make them all eat
your dust. Cast your lot in with votes, with
electoral smarts: the chance to win hearts
and wallets, to tilt the whole table, tip cash
spinning rich to your pockets, sneak pennies
from sinks and from garrets to bolster your
highest turrets. Oh yes, that's the game,
that's the play, your great focus. So master
the anthem, suit up and bow deep: you'll
be raking it in, like a boss, in your sleep.

13. Night Terrors

'Le pas cessa, pourquoi?' (The footsteps stopped. Why?) — *Mallarmé*

In the middle of the night? Yes of course, you
bet. At the point, the very minute you're fretting
on your death, guessing your path to the hearse –
it's then, when you've set your face to the end, that
the sound you'd not even heard is gone: those
footsteps tapping out a pattern on the street,
tracking their way back and forth at the gate. But
now? Not a whisper, not a peep. So all hope of
sleep is forthwith done, as this new-spun silence
stings your fears into fresh bouts of shivering and

fright. Who is it, out there, listening in the dark –
breath-held and lurking, stoking you fast to the
near edge of screaming? What beast is there
haunching, feral, by the door, ready to take out
your throat with one claw, when — shot from your
bed and slid down the stairs — you open a window
barely a hair, to ensure that those footsteps were
nothing and no-one…just ghosts in your head. So,

hunch up; stay still. Best pull the sheets tight.
There are hours yet to wait for relief, for the light.